D0610860

MANGLISH

For Inger and Charles

MANGLISH
WHATEVER HAPPENED
TO OUR LANGUAGE

by
HAROLD (HAITCH) SCRUBY
with
SIMON BLACKALL

Illustrations by Patrick Cook

Collins
Publishers
Australia

Acknowledgements
The authors would like to give particular thanks to Kate
Foord, James Lambert and Diane Wallis for their assistance
in researching this epic work and also to Harry Williamson,
Richard Ackland and David Brunches for their valuable criti-
cisms and contributions.

COLLINS PUBLISHERS AUSTRALIA

First published in 1989 by William Collins Pty Ltd.,
55 Clarence Street, Sydney NSW 2000

Created and Produced by
The Watermark Press, 72-80 Cooper Street,
Surry Hills, NSW 2010, Australia

Copyright © The Watermark Press 1989
Text © Harold Scruby and Simon Blackall
Cartoons © Patrick Cook

National Library of Australia
Cataloguing-in-Publication data:
Scruby, Harold.
    Manglish.
    ISBN 0 7322 2584 1.
    1. English language — Australia — Humor. I. Cook
    Patrick, 1949-   . II. Title.
427'.994

Typeset in Isbell Medium by Sabagraphics, New Zealand.
Printed by The Bookprinter, Melbourne.

Contents

Introduction 7
Foreword 9
Neologisms 11
Tautologies & Redundancies 19
Click go the Clichés 31
Chuck Talk 55
Buzz Words 63
Mixed Metaphors 67
Contradictions 73
Catachreses & Malapropisms 79
Accents 87
Finishing a Sentence 89
Answering your own Question 91
Euphemisms 93
Woolliness 103
Extended Metaphors 107
General Manglish 109

PHILLIP SWALLOWS HIS FIRST FLY

Introduction

In a former life, I of course lived in France. *The* land of inflexibility. You've got to admire them. They've been at war with practically everyone, yet they're still dictators. They revel in their form of speak. They like it so much they resist changing it. I like that. Inflexibility. Passive aggression.

English is a mongrel. And we keep letting it reproduce. It's getting mongrel-er and mongrel-er. Americans (who abandoned any form of real communication some years back) talk of 'momentarily', referring to *when* not *how long.* So, consequently, they've lost the use of the word. The French would not allow that to happen. One would be sent to Conventry (England) if one did that. And no women before you go, either.

In Australia (Mongrel II), we're losing the words "might", "may", and "can". We can no longer say "You can go even though you might not want to, but your father said you definitely may not". Try mucking around with those words and you're in trouble. The fact that *usage* has ruined their meaning does not justify the acceptance of error. But look in some dictionaries. An absolute acceptance. Bastards.

So, I'm not really a pedant, I'm just saddened at our corporate loss. We are not stepping forward. We are slowly falling over.

Before Scruby starts his book, here are a few other observations. They either amuse or annoy, depending on my mood, or who says them.

7

nucular; inequitous; preformance; bress; capsicun; medium strip; regulee; pleese; characterture; coop; vicky verca; video; cd (for the machine); fwee; sumfink; anyfink; chaise lounge; essetera.

If you still think it just *doesn't matter* try getting to a position where you have to write a memoranda. Nothing lasts longer or makes more people laugh than a poor use of language.

But then again, we've got to laugh, don't we?

Clive Alexander Robertson
(spinster of this parish)

Foreword

About five years ago I started to take an active interest in what was happening to our language. I think my brain was jogged by one of those unconscious witticisms made by some lazy speaker who described the nature (or median) strip in the middle of the road as a 'medium strip'. I had visions of a striptease artist taking off some of her clothes for the benefit of passing motorists. It certainly gave me a laugh at the time and with the aid of friends and a mention in Leo Schofield's column in the Sydney Morning Herald, I had soon collected an enormous number of misspelt, mispronounced and certainly misunderstood words. All these were put into a small book which was called WAYNESPEAK. We were probably thinking of cowboys when we named the book so I should apologise to anyone called Wayne who read the book and took offence. Anyway the book turned out to be a minor best-seller and on discussing it in media interviews and with friends we soon began to talk about the many other ways in which our language is being changed, abused and generally mangled. Most of this verbal carnage is undoubtedly caused by the electronic media, the effect of which is to make it increasingly possible for a person to go through life without having to read or write. Another cause is certainly the glorification of the mediocre; the determination to find the lowest common denominator of speech and to establish this as the norm. The results are a tragicomedy of a new language predominantly inflicted on us by politicians, sports commentators and rock singers, all determined to speak to us in our own new tongue.

Certainly it was never the tongue of our mothers!

Alas these perpetrators of 'Manglish' (for that is what they speak) are difficult to attack. They intrude from the sound waves and on to our video screens from secret and probably bomb-proof studios thousands of kilometres away. There they read their lines from cue cards which are written by Manglish gnomes and projected on to transparent glass screens so the masses will not discover the language deficiencies of the speaker. If only we could interject their bumbling lines with cries of 'mixed metaphor', 'tautology' or 'cliché'. Then we might make these 'manglers' of our language pause for thought. The war of course is lost. The Manglers have won. But before we yield completely, spare an hour with us to savour some of the greater lunacies of their speech, for you dear reader, may even yet decide to take up the cudgel in the defence of our language.

Harold (Haitch) Scruby

Neologisms

Unremarkably, languages either grow or they die. The ancient Greek and Roman languages have both ceased to be spoken except in the mystifying process of religion. So too have the languages of the Minoans, the Celts, many Aboriginal tribes and most of the north American Indians. Our language on the contrary is growing at a startling pace.

In the two years since the Oxford English Dictionary was last updated, an additional 5000 words have come into the language! Rest assured that this figure is well on the low side compared with the huge quantity of new words available to the lexicographers.

Every hour of every day we are inundated with 'new speak', with jargon and with 'bafflegab', that perfect word coined by Douglas Adams. The Americans, particularly those in the advertising industry, seem to lead in this department.

There was a huge leap in the number of new words when the Nixon administration took office in Washington. The new government was largely made up of Californians determined to show how modern they were. Perhaps it was because they needed to demonstrate their skill with words in what one might describe as audio circus acts. This usually meant turning nouns into verbs but almost any new form of language seemed acceptable provided it was spoken with conviction. Australians needless to say were quick to come up with their own inventive speech.

The person who receives a broadside of 'newspeak' is probably so keen to understand that he or she will nod in assent and adopt the same word at a later meeting. Let us make up an example. Take the word tabletop. We all understand its meaning. It is a noun. It describes a physical part of a table. But then one day at a business meeting it starts its transformation into a verb. The perpetrator, maybe a banker, advertising man, property developer or whoever, announces to the assembly that it is time the other members stop talking vaguely about their proposals, take them out of their briefcases and put them on the top of the table, so everyone can see. But that is not what he says. Because he is as modern as tomorrow he cannot use clear understandable English. To do so would 'downplay' his position, his skills, his aura. So he uses newspeak. His actual words are: 'OK gentlemen let's tabletop our ideas.' Nobody shrieks with laughter. Nobody smiles. Everyone understands. They say nothing.

Two days later they are back in their own offices and recount what happened at the meeting. 'Fred Katzenbach had us tabletop our ideas', they say and already the new verb *to tabletop* has increased its usage by 600%. But don't imagine that our new verb will lie dormant for several years. The proposals which Fred made them all tabletop were for a new low-cost housing development and there is to be a media release. A radio journalist hears about the meeting and suddenly the new verb has been used on an audience of millions. Two months later President Bush in a TV interview syndicated worldwide, announces that he is still waiting for Mikhail Gorbachev to tabletop his proposals. Fred has subconciously made history and we need a new dictionary.

Here are just a few examples of neologisms, many of which we have dared to interpret for their real meanings. When you hear someone using one, try asking the speaker what he or she means. They will look at you blankly and you must disarm them by smiling back like Mona Lisa. Your task is done.

13

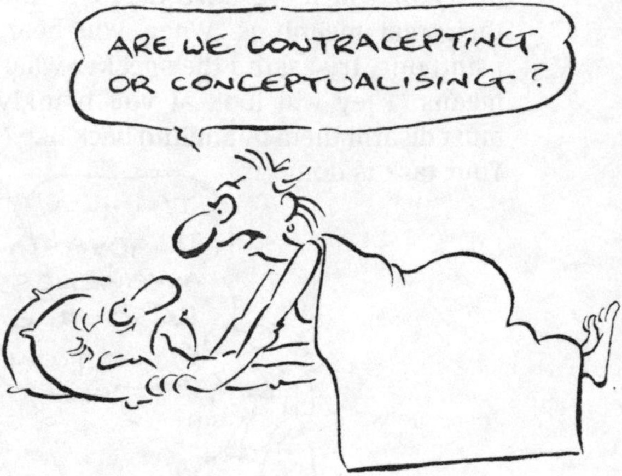
ARE WE CONTRACEPTING OR CONCEPTUALISING?

to access

to auralise

to bankroll

to best (I bested him at squash)

to boomerang

to bottom line

to carpet

to ceiling (the prices ceilinged around June)

to cold shoulder (he's been cold-shouldering him all week)

to concrete (we hope this will concrete our relationship)

to contemporise

to contracept (he had no idea of contracepting)

to corporatise

to diagram (can you diagram this document for me?)

to dollarise

to evidence (this is evidenced by this document)

to expense

to expertise (guess!)

to eyeball

to green light (to give approval)

to guest (a programme)

to impact

to leverage

to keyboard (can you keyboard this in please?)

to marginalise

to matrix e.g. hear Charlie just got matrixed = there has been a reorganisation as a result of which Charlie has been fired

to party (come on, let's party)

to personalise

to plateau

to position

to prioritise

to profile (there was a story profiling her in the paper)

to schematise

to showcase

to snowball (interest rates snowballed this month)

to source (can you source these documents?)

to springboard (that springboarded me into my career)

to task (we're getting someone to task that right away)

to tenant (we've tenanted the place for six months)

to verbalise (to put into words)

to video (can you video that for me?)

to vocalise

to workshop (let's workshop the problem)

to waste (kill; destroy)

Tautologies and Redundancies

This is the greatest breeding ground for Manglish. It is here that politicians and priests, sports commentators and corporate leaders all sink proudly into the mire, blissfully unaware of their excesses. Indeed so great is their hubris that they are not averse to repeating their charming little errors in the correct belief that repetition can only reinforce the strength of their words. A tautology needless to say, is a repetition of an idea or statement but often using other words.

Here are some true tautological babblings and redundant rabbitings covering a wide range of subjects but, you may note, with a large emphasis on sport.

I'm going to make a prediction — it could go either way.

Or as another commentator put it, thereby affecting a subtle change in meaning
I really expect it to go one way or the other tonight.

ISAAC NEWTON DISCOVERS TAUTOLOGY

And seen from the competitor's view
*I hope to come first or second, or at least
win it.*

The fierceness of such a performance may well
have brought on this superb piece of
commentary
He did a lot of running with his legs today.

Not that that got him very far
*He's missed two caught and bowled
opportunities — both off his own bowling.*

And who was he anyway?
*If I keep getting Boyd and O'Grady mixed up
it's because they look so alike, particularly
around the head.*

And here is a mind-boggling statistic from
another commentator:
*The stadium is close to capacity — as far as
full is concerned . . .*

But there is nothing like a simple positive
outlook, and here sports commentators seem to
excel
*If we were talking positively, I can't see no
reason why Christie can't get a medal.*

Or
*Of course one of Stephen Hendry's greatest
assets is his ability to score when he's
playing.*

Or
A boxer makes a comeback for one of two reasons: either he's broke, or he needs the money.

Or
Here he is. Yesterday's winner. The man who won yesterday.

Or simply
It was a goal of really simple simplicity.

Then there was the sprinter who told us:
My personal best time

And one final word from our competitors
We're very pleased about the way we played because we know we can play like that.

Right. Now we can get away from sport to the one or two examples we found from other fields
London isn't the largest city, but its definitely larger than the next largest.

And what is the best way to appreciate this vast metropolis?
You have only to fly over it, or go in a helicopter.

And from a Sydney meteorologist . . .
Its been raining for eight consecutive days in a row.

But perhaps one of the most frequent and unconscious tautologies of all is the phrase
I'm going to go

One famous political leader announced after an election:
We didn't win and we didn't lose

And another well-known politician who had an unenviable reputation for tautologies came up with the following:
It's all summed up in the crux of one situation.

and

Queensland is not prepared to put its feet on the sticking paper and be stuck with it.

and
We stick like glue and we work like glue.

and
We won't be able to sit on uranium. Firstly because it would not be right and secondly because it would be wrong.

Other utterances of the great man included:
We have to get the status quo back to what it was before.

and
The secret of my success is that I don't beat around the bush and say exactly what I mean.

There are many other tautologies, admittedly less spectacular, which have found a permanent home in our language. Here is an extended example of what we mean.

It is my subjective opinion, but, nevertheless one which I think represents the general consensus, that access should be restricted to members only. The alternative choice, but not the more preferable one, is to abolish membership altogether and charge an entrance fee of some reasonable amount of money. After all, we don't want any Tom, Dick or Harry, and I suppose now I should add Brenda to that list of names, being able to just walk in here off the street. And I'm sure each and every one of you feels the same. Am I right?

The following are just some of the tautologies which are daily occurrences. Believe us.

the actual thing itself

and etc

announce orally

around about
6 pm in the evening

as near as near

back back straight into another car

the Bargain Basement downstairs

circle around the block

collaborate together
come back again
the current climate at the moment
debate about
different varieties
each of you individually
an essential prerequisite
exactly the same thing
the extra thing I have added is
a family heirloom
filthy dirty pig
final upshot

26

forward progress
free gifts
further additions
future prospects
grateful thanks
greetings and salutations
I have experienced this before
I used to do that before
I'll just clean up the mess
in a row one after another
internationally around the world
it gave me some bad adverse effects
it was cut into two halves
its re-echoed
I've been here since we first founded the company
join together in unison
kills flies and cockies dead
last will and testament
lob the ball high up into the air
male bachelor
man-made synthetic
male penis

mix together

the mural on the wall

my ancestors were original First Fleeters

my own car

nationally around Australia

never once

new novelty

null and void

old out-dated material

one and the same

the other alternative

overseas imports

past history

a preliminary preamble

pregnant with child

preset

raging out of control

recall back

reduce down

repay back

reiterate again

repeat again

restate again

returning for a comeback

reverse backwards

right now at this moment/point in time

so incredible I could scarce believe it

stupid idiot

sufficient enough

the sum total

tediously boring

there's no need for undue worry

toxic poisons

a true fact

12 midnight

12 noon

a unique, never to be repeated, offer

a wholly new innovation

the yearly AGM (annual general meeting)

very true

Click go
the Clichés

A favourite of all Manglish speakers is the cliché. There is nothing really wrong in using a cliché. We all drop them into our conversation from time to time and in many cases the use of the cliché is our immediate short cut to convey meaning. However the current tendency, particularly for our politicians, is to speak in one long stream of clichés. But just what is a cliché? Surely there are millions of words and expressions which we all repeat? Of course there are, but not all of them are clichés. A cliché is a phrase or expression which is worn out by overuse. As the late Hollywood mogul Sam Goldwyn is reported to have said: "Can't we have some new cliches?" The meaning a cliché conveys is not necessarily worthless but the style is oh so predictable and oh so boring! In the Manglish *Cliché of the Year Competition* which we shall obviously be forced to hold as a sequel to the Manglish *Mixed Metaphor of the Year Competition*, the phrase "to open up Pandora's box" must surely be well on the way to number one spot. However since the entries are likely to be myriad, we have decided to divide them into three categories.

Cliché Category I The Overworked Phrase

For this section we have collected some choice examples and put them into a nice little paragraph. Everyone is free to use it without charge the next time it is their turn to speak in a Parliamentary debate on the economy.

Be that as it may, when we arrive bright-eyed and bushy tailed at the meeting, determined to rock the boat; the opposition is sure to batten down the hatches. As they beat a hasty retreat you can bet your bottom dollar they'll go straight back to the drawing board and come up with a brand spanking new idea that is really only a shot in the dark but one which they hope will allow them to depart from the scene in a blaze of glory.

And there are plenty more where they came from.

all in a day's work

all things being equal

the best thing since sliced bread

better late than never

*the bigger they are the harder they
fall*

blood is thicker than water

the bottom line

boys will be boys

burn the midnight oil

*clear, concise and straight to the
point*

conspicuous by one's absence

a dose of your own medicine

easier said than done

far be it for me

flattery will get you nowhere

for all intents and purposes

from the bottom of my heart

God has given you a special gift

going around in circles

a heart of gold

I know how you must feel

I'd give my right arm for it

in a blue funk

in a word

it's all a matter of taste

just like mother used to make

keep your shirt on

last but not least

lay down the law

let's get the show on the road

life wasn't meant to be easy

like I need a hole in the head

live and learn

live and let live

lock, stock and barrel

long in the tooth

love's eternal triangle

maintain the status quo

a matter of life and death

misery loves company

moment of truth

the moment you've all been waiting for

money doesn't grow on trees

A FELL SWOOP

more than meets the eye

neither hide nor hair of

no rest for the wicked

not with a bang but a whimper

off the beaten track

on one's last legs

on your bike

one fell swoop

out of sight, out of mind

pinpoint accuracy

point of no return

possession is nine tenths of the law

the powers that be

put your money where your mouth is

ride roughshod over

road to perdition

saving for a rainy day

second to none

see light at the end of the tunnel

he would give you the shirt off his
back

short and sweet

a shoulder to cry on

the show must go on

a sight for sore eyes

sign of the times

slave over a hot stove

stark raving mad

that's life

that's the way the cookie crumbles

there's no business like show business

thick and fast

thick as thieves

through thick and thin

till my dying day

to cut a long story short

to the best of my ability

too good to be true

too much of a good thing

trip the light fantastic

what's a nice girl like you doing in a place like this

when all is said and done

when I was young

whisper sweet nothings in one's ear

the whole kit and caboodle

with all due respect

with bated breath

you can't win 'em all

you took the words right out of my mouth

Cliché Category II The Threadbare Quotation/Proverb

This is the easiest to detect. Whereas the overused phrase of the first category "can slip under your cover" in the endless drone of political debate, the threadbare quotation/proverb is far more easily detected. The problem is that the major users of these clichés are convinced that they are displaying great erudition while conveying their often very simple message. Once again we are providing you with a flexible and reusable paragraph in case you are suddenly called to speak in Parliament.

And so madam speaker, just as night follows day, it goes without saying that we are reaping the unjust rewards of the opposition having opened a Pandora's box out of which jumped a new semi-government body which grew like Topsy. Being full of the milk of

human kindness (I refer to yours truly of course) I had declined to mention the matter before now, but in view of their below the belt attack on my friend, the honourable member for Burrumbuttock, I am forced to reply.

Just in case you are called upon to speak on an obscure and little discussed issue which the above paragraph doesn't quite address, here is a list of relevant phrases which will get you out of any tight spot. Remember, the more you use the less you commit yourself.

all things must pass

all's fair in love and war

an apple a day keeps the doctor away

beauty is in the eye of the beholder

a bird in the hand is worth two in the bush

blood, sweat and tears

cast pearls before swine

don't count your chickens before they hatch

the early bird catches the worm

a fool and his money are soon parted

a friend in need is a friend indeed

frailty thy name is woman

the fruits of one's labours

go ahead, make my day

hell hath no fury like a woman scorned

hope springs eternal

it never rains but it pours

labour of love

land of milk and honey

lend an ear

lie back and think of England

like two ships passing in the night
a miss is as near as a mile
more sinned against than sinning
necessity is the mother of invention
neither a borrower nor a lender be
no man is an island
patience is a virtue
a picture paints a thousand words

42

a pound of flesh

the proof of the pudding is in the eating

the slings and arrows of outrageous fortune

still waters run deep

survival of the fittest

44

there, but for the grace of God, go I

there's something fishy going on around here

time immemorial

time heals all wounds

time waits for no man

to thine own self be true

truth is stranger than fiction

truth will out

two's company, three's a crowd

the tyranny of distance

water under the bridge

when in Rome

without further ado

worth one's weight in gold

would to God I could be with you

Cliché Category III The Frayed Figure of Speech

Figures of speech are often identified by being prefaced by the word "as" followed by an example. Frequently they are used for a brief period and then dropped in favour of the next event-related cliché. The example which follows is suitable for use in situations as varied as council meetings, church assemblies, fund raising occasions and state parliamentary sessions.

It took a weight off my mind when the Grim Reaper waltzed in with flying colours just as the rosy-fingered dawn was creeping over the roof tops. It was the fickle finger of fate finding a cold hearth to sit by during the long day's journey into night.

The following are just some of many useful figures of speech. By inserting the odd conjunction, preposition or any of those other linking words, you can form a two-minute speech, handy for debating, impromptu addresses and for that little lull in the dinner party conversation.

as fate would have it

I smell a rat

I'll give you a piece of my mind

it's a dog's life

it's a small world

just the tip of the iceberg
go over with a fine tooth comb
lap of luxury
let it all hang out
let one's imagination run wild
life and soul of the party
life is just a bowl of cherries
life's a bitch, and then you die
like a bat out of hell
a load off my mind
make a mountain out of a mole hill
milk of human kindness
move heaven and earth
my heart bleeds for you
my lips are sealed
on the spur of the moment
once in a blue moon
par for the course
pillar of society
play your cards right
quick as a wink
rock the boat
runs in the blood

sands of time

seize the bull by the horns

a shot in the dark

skating on thin ice

the sky is the limit

snake in the grass

snug as a bug in a rug

strike while the iron is hot

that takes the cake

that's a whole new ball game

that's the name of the game

there are plenty more fish in the ocean/sea

there is more than one way to skin a cat

thick as thieves

tie the knot

toe the line

tower of strength

turning in her/his grave

ugly as sin

until hell freezes over

until the cows come home

warm the cockles of your heart

work one's fingers to the bone

your blood is worth bottling

However, before you give yourself totally and entirely free rein with our comprehensive selection of clichés and begin to make fascinating and interesting speeches any time you feel the urge coming on, you should read the following passage carefully.

I should like to read or hear, just once, about tacks that aren't brass, questions that aren't moot, coasts that aren't clear, fates that aren't worse than death, and a mean that isn't golden.

And, just once, a null without a void, a might without a main, a far without a wide, a six of one without a half-dozen of the other, tooth without a nail, and ways without means.

And, just once, an unfit fiddle, a warm cucumber, a young hill, a stupid owl, a hard impeachment, a black elephant, a sage's paradise, feet of gold, the pepper of the earth, an unbloated plutocrat, and a sad Lothario.

And, just once, a social caterpillar, Father Nature, the orange of one's eye, an uncracked dawn, a picture of illness, ignorance after the event, a tower of weakness, an unsure slowness, a low dryness, and a lively earnestness.

And, just once, a fair without a square, a safe without a sound, a sackcloth without ashes, a wear without a tear, a fast without a loose, a rack without a ruin, a kill without a cure, a long without a short, and a storm without a port.

And, just once, a merciless errand, an ungrieved error, an unpsychological moment, a light horse, a live certainty, an indecisive effect, an embarrassment of poverty, an eternal quadrangle, an emaciated calf, and someone who has been frightened into his wits.

And, just once, a nail that isn't hit on the head, a feather that can't knock you down, a gift that doesn't come from the gods, a bad Samaritan, a delicate exaggeration, and a pin that doesn't drop.

And, just once, an ungilded lily, good dirty fun, tepid congratulations, a wagon hitched to a meteorite, something that costs an ugly penny, someone who is gone and forgotten, and someone who would go through fire but not through water.

And, just once, a hue without a cry, a hem without a haw, a hit without a miss, a hither without a yon, a head without a shoulders, a spick without a span, a hammer without a tongs, fish on a string or a net or a pan but not in a kettle, a prophet with honor, and purely without simply.

And, just once, sweet grapes, soft facts, an unpicked bone, a tempest in a coffeepot, a ducksong or a goosesong but not a swansong, a bull that is taken by the tail, and a rhinestone in the rough.

Sydney J Harris *A Pretty Kettle of Clichés*

Chuck Talk

American and Australian English are often combined to produce something totally foreign to comprehensible English. We have decided to give it a name — Chuck Talk.

This new language which is an integral part of Manglish is creeping insidiously into the Australian idiom. It is no longer rare to hear sentences where verbs are absent, important words are left out and superfluous ones added. Where nouns are turned into verbs and verbs are turned into nouns. Where subjects are rare and participles have a life of their own. Such misuse can have a number of effects on a person, including chronic depression and cerebral haemorrhage. So be careful. You may like to pause halfway through the following list. Have a coffee. Take a walk. "Lay" down. Before it all gets on top of you . . .

Here are just a few examples

airplane
aeroplane

A-okay
all right

appetiser
entrée

a ways down the track
a distance

bathroom
lavatory

beat up
knocked about

blooper
TV blunder

blow someone away
kill someone by shooting

blow someone's mind
amaze

bonk
copulate

buddy
mate

bulk
lots of

bummer
a bad thing

the can/john/head
the toilet/lavatory

chew out
criticise

cockamaimy
crazy; stupid

do dinner
have dinner

do drugs
take drugs

dude
bloke

the exact same thing
exactly the same thing

fanny-pack
bum-bag (skiing)

58

gas
petrol

get off of the bus
get off the bus

gotten
got

happening
exciting (a really happening place)

hassle
worry

have a nice day
good-bye

he dove into the pool
he dived into the pool

he's bad news
he's trouble

I'll come by your house
I'll come to your house

I'll call you
I'll ring you

I'll write you
I'll write to you

in back of the house
behind the house

ketchup
tomato sauce

lay down
lie down

make a right
turn right

no can do
sorry, I can't

one hundred sixty two
one hundred and sixty two

pay phone
public telephone

pig out
make a glutton of oneself

rage
have a good time

right here
here

right now
now

right there
there

rubber
condom

take care
good-bye

totally awesome
amazing

touch base
meet

trunk
boot (of a car)

yonks
a long time

zilch
nothing

zit
pimple

Buzz Words

In our youth we were taught that less was more, that simplicity meant clarity and that short words were often more easily understood than long ones. Most of us would like to think that this still holds true but there is a determined body of people whose livelihoods apparently depend on their ability to make the language seem more difficult than it really is. Here are a few of these words and for some of them we have attempted to provide a translation. They may be wrong. But remember, you can always ask the speakers exactly what they mean and if they know they may be able to enlighten you. The chances are of course that they don't know and will be grateful for your assistance in translating their adopted language.

articulate
speak

at this point in time
now

back-to-back
continuous

build opportunity
develop an idea

come on stream
to start

cutting edge
activity (work)

decision-making process
deciding

down the gurgler
lost

down the track
later

electronic mail
message sent by computer

fast track(ing)
going forward quickly

in this day and age
now

interfacing
interacting

is in place
exists, is ready

network building
making friends

orientate
to face East

raw data
facts and figures

scenario
outline of the plot

take on board
to adopt

up and running
in operation

user-friendly
easy to use

window of opportunity
chance

RAW DATA

66

Mixed Metaphors

This is a surprisingly common event. A metaphor is usually a nice short figure of speech in which a descriptive term is used to convey an idea. However it does this by using an example that is often far removed from reality. That is to say we use an analogy. Let us take an example. *To bark up the wrong tree*. Simply and perhaps more boringly put, we are applying our energies in the wrong direction. The analogy is that we are like a dog which has chased some prey up a tree but is wasting his energy because he has mistaken the tree up which his prey went. When we mix our metaphors the results are often very funny. Often the mixture occurs because the speaker subconsciously believes that the actual metaphor is too short and therefore tries to improve it. When a well-known racing personality was asked the date of a particular event, he replied that *off the cuff of my head* he was unable to give the answer. What he meant to say of course was either *off the cuff* or *off the top of my head*. But what he did in fact was to extend the metaphor and in effect doubled it. His thinking was muddled and he was quite unaware how funny he was.

Here then are some good examples of mixed metaphors produced by politicians, sports commentators, lawyers and others. We have not identified the authors but believe us, they do exist!

Some of the best come from well-known Queensland politicians who should be charged with Manglishing in the first degree. Several superlative offerings have come straight from our revered television commentators and a few have come from as far away as Britain, Ireland and the United States.

The following confused offering gives rise to visions of someone writing their signature on a large bell:
By that stage the death knell had been signed

And the author of the next piece was presumably describing the hottest robot on the block:
There's a heart of steel burning inside him

For restructuring the human body, another commentator is heading for first prize with his little offering:
They've got old shoulders on their heads

And this person obviously felt that one was not enough and went on to double-up on his metaphor count with:
Everything under the sun that walks on two legs and hasn't got a party of its own is in the ALP

Others assert that eggs are really made of milk, probably because the nursery rhyme illustrator had suffered deprivation in his youth:
Once the milk has been spilt in this sort of case it's very difficult to put Humpty Dumpty back on the wall again

A prominent Queenslander (who obviously lives in a land where trees frequently serve beer) must have been trying to help a blind friend when he said:
You are barking up a dry tree

But it was definitely an Englishman who said:
We've got to sit down and have a think where we stand

And it was probably a lady from Wellington who felt it necessary to extend her metaphor in a most forgivable way when she said:
They're hanging on to their hats for grim life

The hotter the climate, the more frequently politicians chose cold analogies, as with this extended metaphor from one of the prime exponents of Manglish
It's no good putting a wet blanket over wages and prices, because that's only the tip of the iceberg

And what visionary came up with the gem:
It's dog eat dog in this rat race

The author of this mixed metaphor displays either a total lack of geography or the determination to avoid all local food. Presumably one can buy spaghetti almost anywhere these days.

When you are in Korea, you have to eat as the Romans do

The following is an excellent example of confused and mixed metaphors, not to mention misunderstood words. It has probably been elaborated since the original statement, reputedly made by an 18th century Irish politician. It is a classic.

Mr Speaker, I smell a rat. I see it floating in the air; and if it is not nipped in the bud, it will burst forth into a terrible conflagration that will deluge the world.

More recently another politician talked about:

. . . the unravelling of the Tory economic miracle which is turning into a mirage.

An English (woman) radio commentator came up with a mixture of two of the most frequently used metaphors, both connected with food:

That's the gravy on the cake.

And her efforts are only eclipsed by another commentator, whose first name was Wally, who said:

I wish I'd had the hot-dog concession — they'd have sold like hot cakes.

For transmogrification, followed by amazing dexterity with hooves, we have this offering from an interview on the BBC:

He has been made a sacrificial lamb for taking the lid off a can of worms.

A British politician, who obviously has a military background, seems not only to have mixed his metaphors but made them contradictory too:

Certain elements of the BMA leadership have gone over the top and taken fully entrenched positions.

But what about:
He's come on in fits and bounds.

And how is this for a description of the Department of Social Security:
. . . a backwater clogged with hot potatoes

The young barrister who uttered this plea for justice actually won the case:
If my learned friend is right, there will be dug a bottomless pit that will forever hang over the head of my client.

At a scientific meeting one scientist accused a colleague of:
trying to bolster up the scaffolding of a collapsing hypothesis with a red herring.

And a last word from a politician:
You can lead a horse to the river, but you can't make him water.

Contradictions

One way to judge a really good contradiction is the level of confusion which it produces in yourself and those around you. Reading arms policy statements issued by the President of the United States or other pacifists is a good way to find the highest possible level of continuous contradiction. (Your brain may even start to melt.) Once you have established this, however, you must begin to look for more subtle ways in which people tell you nothing over a long period of time, or over a short period of time. We have provided examples from all of these categories, beginning with some words from a well-known political campaigner.

They only care for their own policies. Well, I'll not campaign or advocate any policies but my own.

And now for a perfect example:
We intend to uphold the rights of the individual. If they want to march up Queen Street, disrupt all the traffic, stop the legitimate comings and goings of people, we simply won't let them do it.

The following contradiction must surely come
from an astronaut:
**The wheels are not off, we're going down the
road. We're in orbit.**

But consider this one:
**Moreton Island will be rehabilitated after
the mining people have been there in such a
way you won't recognise it.**

Quite so! Now let's hear from a gentleman
who is probably absolutely right in
using the following description. We may be
stretching things to include this as a
contradiction but it does make us wonder . . .
**There goes Kevin Borovich, the Yugoslavian
Maori from North Auckland.**

And from another sports commentator:
The wind was completely still.

And during a cricket match . . .
**It's only a light shower, or a downpour
really.**

And then . . .
Margaret Kelly, you were born an orphan.

And
**I have always been more mature than I
actually am.**

A British commentator called Jim assured us that:
The crowd's been let in free today and they're certainly getting their money's worth.

While at the Grand Prix circuit we were informed that:
He is almost definitely in a class of his own with Prost.

And at Wimbledon we were told:
He's an impeccable player, but sometimes he still makes mistakes.

And more tennis contradictions:
That was a precise shot, yet with a little too much over-correction so that it just went out.

Some news commentators can even bring people back from the dead . . .
Australia's latest shark fatality, who miraculously survived.

And a final word from an Australian tennis commentator:
She forces her opponents to make unforced errors.

Algie Wyatt, a character in Shirley Hazzard's **People in Glass Houses**, works for the United Nations as a translator. Every so often he looks up from his desk and says 'Got one'.
'What?' asked Lidia Korabetski, looking up from the passage she was translating.

'Contradiction in terms.' Algie was collecting contradictions in terms: to a nucleus of 'military intelligence' and 'competent authorities' he had added such discoveries as the soul of efficiency, easy virtue, enlightened self-interest, Bankers Trust, and Christian Scientist.

'What?' Lidia asked again.

'Cultural mission,' replied Algie, turning the page and looking encouraged, as if he studied the document solely for such rewards as this.

And to round off this section may we leave you with two frequently used terms which surely must be contradictory:

Peace-keeping force
Limited nuclear war

Catachreses and Malapropisms

A catachresis is a misapplication of a word. Some of these are very common and have been occurring for decades, even centuries. Others are relatively recent, but common amongst speakers of English. A few are one-off coinages by people grappling with the language.

Malapropisms are best defined by quoting from their originator, Mrs Malaprop, in Sheridan's ***The Rivals***. Accused of decking ***'. . . her dull chat with hard words which she don't understan'***, she replies ***'Sure, if I reprehend anything in this world, it is the use of my oracular tongue, and a nice derangement of epitaphs.'***

airzone layer
ozone layer

antidotes
anecdotes

anti-semantic
anti-Semitic

ascetic
aesthetic

battle an eyelid
bat an eyelid

chaffing at the bit
champing at the bit

continually
continuously

continuously
continually

cup of chino
cappuccino

curve
kerb

depository
suppository

double ammonia
double pneumonia

dry reaching
dry retching

earsdropping
eavesdropping

Edifice complex
Oedipus complex

the entranced families
the entrenched families

exerts
excerpts

fettucine with harlot sauce
fettuccine with shallot sauce

flaunt
flout

for all intensive purposes
for all intents and purposes

happy as a larry
happy as Larry/ as a lark

humbrage
umbrage

inter-gestion
indigestion

Lesbianese
Lebanese

macandamien nuts
macadamia nuts

mute point
moot point

obnoxious weed
noxious weed

off her own back
off her own bat

old timers' disease
Alzheimer's disease

orgasm
organism

plutonic
platonic

$10
FOR
FIVE
MINUTES

SUCKING PIG

82

proprietary
propriety

prostrate
prostate

reality
realty

reconnaissance
recognizance

sheath
sheaf

skylark
sky light

slithers of beef
slivers of beef

squash
quash

suckling pig
sucking pig

testicles
tentacles

title wave
tidal wave

transcendental medication
transcendental meditation

vagrancies of the situation
vagaries of the situation

Vitaminese
Vietnamese

watercrest
watercress

water on a duck's back
water off a duck's back

Westminister
Westminster

A well-known cricket commentator fell into the old trap when he informed viewers:
He's amphibious in the field — he throws with both hands.

and someone at the Olympics stunned us with:
Look at the boxer from Guacamole (Guatemala) go!

travellers at Sydney airport are bound to leap into action when they read:
Please report this toilet running to any Ansett staff.

and, as we have already mentioned, the politicians are always ready to calm matters down when they say:
Don't let's jump to confusions.

all hair and no liability seems to be the way to handle fragile antiques as someone said:
Be careful of these — they're family hair looms.

and who was the sporting great who said:
One day I'll get someone to write my autobiography.

Never mind, the newspapers always get it right as did the *Sydney Morning Herald* sub-editor who came up with the line:
The Fitzgerald Report will serve as an epithet to the Bjelke-Petersen years in Queensland.

Accents

This book is about the breakdown of the English language and not about accents and inflexions in speech. However sometimes an accent can cause confusion. Everyone has some sort of accent but unlike other parts of the English-speaking world such as the United States or Great Britain, an Australian accent is generally difficult to identify as having come from one part of the continent or another. There are however a couple of noticeable exceptions.

Victorians, more so Melburnians, have a propensity to swap the "el" sound for an "al" sound and vice versa. Melbourne thus becomes *Malbourne*, Alfred becomes *Elfred*, television becomes *talavision* and helicopter becomes *halicopter*. Elton/*Alton*; Elvis/*Alvis* and the El Alamein fountain becomes *Al Elamein* fountain. Melburnians are therefore advised not to name their sons Allen or their daughters Ellen if they are ever likely to cross the border or appear on national quiz shows. Of course none of the Victorian readers of this book speaks like this and it is certainly true to say that some of the broadest Australian accents emanate from NSW and Queensland.

South Australians on the other hand sometimes have a propensity to swallow their Ls. *Myrtwle, the schoowlgirwl from Glenewlg who won the*

Gowld Medawl in the hurdwles speaks in an accent developed from postwar English migrants. Finally from across the Tasman we have the phenomenon of the shortened or disappearing vowel. The New Zealand accent frequently gives rise to misunderstandings, sometimes with amusing consequences. Hill becomes ***hull*** or simply ***h'll***, this is ***thus*** and that is ***thet***.

Ask any New Zealand woman what she does about sex at night and she will immediately respond *"We have dunner"*. The final score: ***Austraya sucks, New Z'lund sairvun***. And that ***my fallow Australians***, is enough about accents!

88

Finishing a Sentence

Along with the upward inflexion, Australians have another idiosyncracy of speech when they come to finish a sentence. This is to add a few words for no good reason. The uninitiated may take this to be a gratuitous insult whereas in fact it is almost a sign of endearment. Here are a few examples which you will instantly recognise.

ya know
and that
but
right
okay
like
ay (particularly Queensland and NZ)

Answering your own Questions

Australians have a unique habit of answering their own questions in the one sentence. It presupposes that the person to whom the question or greeting is addressed is either deaf, dumb or both. How many times have you heard the following?

> *'How ya gowen . . . good?'*
> *'Where've ya been . . . to the footie?'*
> *'What's for tea . . . chops?'*
> *'How was Hobart . . . cold?'*

These questions are also usually completed by raising the voice. This upward inflexion is quite common and peculiar to Australia and is particularly noticeable among the young. It appears to indicate a form of uncertainty and possibly apology. In the seventies it seemed to have reached a pure art-form when the use of the upward inflexion was **de rigueur** amongst the Bali-bound brown rice set. The habit has shown signs of waning in recent years.

Euphemisms

For a nation renowned for its rugged individualism and where people are known for their directness in speech, it comes as a surprise to find that in fact we very rarely say what we mean. Far from being the last people to call a spade a spade, we use every verbal device to avoid using the real word for something. We do this lest we offend, appear to be too direct or even perhaps for outdated reasons or prudery. On occasions we use words which will enhance something that is basically dull and make it sound pleasanter or more important. A perfect example is that part of the service station where they give your car a grease and oil change is frequently called a "lubritorium" making it sound an important, even desirable place to visit.

The following are just some of the infinite ways of avoiding using the right word for a situation. We have only given a small selection but doubtless you will have many more of your own:

93

car smash
accident

adultery
extramarital activity; affair

advertisement
break; message (from our sponsor)

argument
domestic

arrest
apprehend

bastard
love child

bisexual
AC/DC; ambidextrous

blind
sight-deprived

body odour
BO

bookie
turf accountant

breasts
boobs; bust

bribe
(noun) commission; contribution;
kickback
(verb) fix

brothel
boarding house; massage parlour

condom
French letter, rubber, sheath

dead
deceased; departed; late (adj);

death
the big sleep; eternal rest

delapidated
handyman's delight; needs some work

dictator
strong man

die
expire; fade away; pass away; fall asleep

drunk
inebriated; light-headed; tiddly; under
the weather

false teeth
dentures

fart
break wind; flatulence

fat
corpulent; cuddly; paunchy; plump

gamble
speculate

garbage collector
sanitary engineer

gardener
landscaper

genitals
private parts; nether regions

homosexual
gay;

housewife
domestic engineer

insurance against death
life insurance

kill
account for; dispatch; dispose of; put
down; put to sleep;

killing
anti-personnel (forces)

lavatory
amenity; convenience; little girls/boys
room

lie
erroneous report; embroider the truth;
fabrication;

lover
companion; friend

masturbation
self-stimulation

menstruation
calendar pains; cramps

mistakes
errata

molest
interfere with

moronic
a couple of bricks short of a load; a couple of sandwiches short of a picnic; simple; not the full quid

naked
au naturel; in the altogether

nuclear war
all-out strategic exchange

old age
golden years

oral sex
cunnilingus; fellatio; soixante-neuf

orgasm
come

penis
tool; dick; willie; prick; cock and many more

poor
disadvantaged; low income earners; underprivileged

porn
adult erotica; sexually explicit;

pregnant
in the family way

prison
correction centre; detention centre

prisoner
detainee; inmate;

promiscuous
swinging; loose

prostitute
call girl; lady of the night; street walker

repress
pacify (esp. policing of crowds)

rough
physical

sacked
discharged; let go; resigned; retrenched

sexual activity
be intimate with; bonking; sleep with;

shoot
exchange bullets

spit
expectorate

steal
misappropriate; help oneself to;
souvenir

stingy
economical; thrifty

tuberculosis
TB

testicles
bollocks; balls; nuts

theft
loss; shrinkage

undertaker
funeral director;

venereal disease
VD; social disease

victim
casualty

war
conflict; involvement; trouble

worker
engineer

worsen
escalate

wrong
questionable

Sometimes people use an all-purpose euphemism as their way of avoiding the real word. They will say we went to the *you know what*, or he used *one of those things* or just mumble something unintelligible and not finish the sentence.

The following are just a few examples:

thingo; thing; blank; beep; blip; censored; adjective; proverbial; what-do-you-call-'em; whatsut; you know what; one of those (and clears the throat)

Woolliness

Another category in which metaphors of both kinds (mixed **and** extended) occur frequently, is woolliness. This can mean anything from unfinished sentences to confusion in word order to what quite obviously is complete stupidity. This makes woolliness quite an easy one to detect. See how you feel after reading just a few of the following, all of which, surprisingly enough, originated somewhere in Queensland.

In talking of astro-physics someone said:
If Flo and I went out of politics there would be such a big black hole and most of you would fall into it as well.

And for one person's children, jet-setting obviously had an entirely different meaning:
Right before the children went to school they'd fly around the State and even down to Brisbane with me, strapped alongside my little single-engined aeroplane.

And
Oh gee, would I change things down there and restore it to what it is meant to be. (On Canberra and himself as Prime Minister)

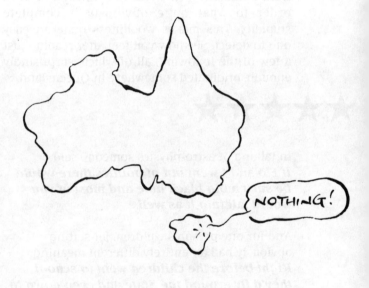

But what on earth does the following mean?
I would like to thank the men and women from all over Queensland who have been working together with their husbands.

Or this!
We're moving in all directions at once.

And
I'm only telling you as I see the situation. I am steeped in politics backwards.

Or
Yes, there are many, many good things in that report, and very, well I suppose difficult to sum up in a few short words like we have today.

And a bit of rhetoric:
What's the difference between an island and the mainland?

But wait for this:
Who wants to stick together with them and get your feet wet. You know, if you get stick foot on sticky paper, you get both of them on, you fall over and Mr Hawke asks us to stick with him. You put your foot on this sticky with him, his and Keating, his Government's got their feet on sticky paper, my word they have.

And finally:
Nothing has been decided yet, don't let's jump to confusions.

Who us? No chance!

But woolliness in speech thrives south of the border as well. It was a Minister in the NSW Government who recently announced:
We have torn up the verbal agreement

Which surely goes to prove the point that it was not worth the paper that it might have been written on. And it was a British Government Minister who came up with the marvelous line:
If you open up that Pandora's Box you never know what Trojan horses will jump out.

Extended Metaphors

Extended metaphors are just ordinary metaphors that are continued by the speaker/writer. They can become very laboured, especially when the relationship is overdone or when the metaphor is more predominant than that which it signifies.

Here are some examples, all of which sound very painful.

If (John) Howard has had his fingers burnt with me, then I have had my legs burnt through him.

and talking of birds of a feather . . .
If you fly with the crows, squawk like a crow and look like a crow, you can't yell out if you get shot at.

or a bit of horse sense . . .
The cold hard facts are that they are flogging a dead horse. It's stiff, hard and cold out there in the paddock and they are standing around with batons and leathers flogging it.

and some thoughts about chariot wheels.

It's been said that the wheels are coming off.
Well I said, you want to watch out because
you'll get run over. The wheels are still on
and it's going and anyone who gets in the
way and tries to stop us, we'll just run them
over.

General Manglish

As we have already seen from the earlier chapters of this great book, Manglish knows no boundaries. It ranges from metaphors to tautologies and euphemisms to contradictions. If we were songwriters instead of aspiring Henry Higginses, we might have come up with something like Cole Porter's wonderful lyrics about changing fashions. So with apologies to the great man our new version runs:

*In former times mistakes in language
were looked upon with mental anguish,
now heaven knows, anything goes!*

The following is a collection of words, malapropisms, mispronunciations and other amazing aspects of language crucifixion which go to make up Manglish. Ask not what your language does for you, but what you can do for your language.

abattor *n.*
abattoir

Aboriginals *n. pl.*
Aborigines

accept *vb.*
except

ackshally *adv.*
actually

advocado *n.*
avocado

agreeance *n.*
agreement

alaminimum *n.*
aluminium

albun *n.*
album

amatcher *adj.*
amateur

ameniable *adj.*
amenable

ampitheatre *n.*
amphitheatre

anenome *n.*
anemone

anethetist *n.*
anaesthetist

angerling *vb.*
angling

antartic *adj.*
antarctic

anythink *n. & pron*
anything

apartide *n.*
apartheid

aquapuncture *n.*
acupuncture

archetypical *adj.*
archetypal

ardamant *adj.*
adamant

arst/arx *vb.*
asked

artheritis *n.*
arthritis

artic *adj.*
arctic

artitect *n.*
architect

ashfelt *n.*
asphalt

asselerate *vb.*
accelerate

assembaly *n.*
assembly

assept/except *vb.*
accept

assessory *n.*
accessory

astericks *n.*
asterisk

athelete *n.*
athlete

Austraya *prop. n.*
Australia

authorative *adj.*
authoritative

balloowuns *n. pl.*
balloons

bassic *adj.*
basic

batter an eyelid *phr.*
bat an eyelid

beholding adj.
beholden

bet to adj.
better

better had phr.
had better

better of phr.
better have

boakay n.
bouquet

boatique n.
boutique

brassiere n.
brasserie

Brisbayne prop. n.
Brisbane

briyant adj.
brilliant

bronichal adj.
bronchial

brureaucracy n.
bureaucracy

burgular n.
burglar

but conj. & adv.
though

buttered to death phr.
battered to death

cabernet savig-non n.
cabernet sauvignon

cameradie n.
camaraderie

Can-berra prop. n.
Canberra

candelstine adj.
clandestine

Cans prop. n.
Cairns

capsicun n.
capsicum

carcogenic adj.
carcinogenic

celry n.
celery

cerebal adj.
cerebral

certainy adv.
certainly

chaise lounge n.
chaise longue

chaffing at the bit phr.
champing at the bit

characterture n.
caricature

chimley *n.*
chimney

choirpractor *n.*
chiropractor

chook *n.*
chicken

Chooseday *n.*
Tuesday

CHOIRPRACTOR

clift *n.*
cliff

close/cloves *n. pl.*
clothes

cockaroach *n.*
cockroach

collary *n.*
colliery

compared to *vb.*
compared with

congradjulations *n. (pl.)*
congratulations

conshume *vb.*
consume

contempry *adj.*
contemporary

continually *adv.*
continuously

contractural *adv.*
contractual

corter/corder *n.*
quarter

could of *vb. (past cond.)*
could have

cruzants/cruzonts *n.*
croissants

cumberbun *n.*
cummerbund

cupe-on *n.*
coupon

cutelry *n.*
cutlery

date-th *n.*
date

daybyou *n.*
debut

definately *adv.*
definitely

deteriate *vb.*
deteriorate

dewarf *n.*
dwarf

diabeets *n.*
diabetes

dias *n.*
dais

different to/than *adj.*
different from

diptheria *n.*
diphtheria

dipthong *n.*
diphthong

EARSDROPPING

118

drawring *n.*
drawing

either do I *phr.*
neither do I

elephantitus *n.*
elephantiasis

entrepeneur *n.*
entrepreneur

eroneous/erogeneous *adj.*
erogenous

escavation *n.*
excavation

esculate *vb.*
escalate

esculator *n.*
escalator

estatic *adj.*
ecstatic

everythink *n.*
everything

exclusitivity *n.*
exclusivity

exerts *n.*
excerpts

exetra/essetera *phr. & n.*
etcetera

expresso n.
espresso

exscape vb.
escape

extra terrestial n.
extra terrestrial

Eyetalian adj.
Italian

fabalous adj.
fabulous

fambly n.
family

fax n. (pl.)
facts

Febuary n.
February

filum n.
film

finickity adj.
pernickety

fith adj.
fifth

fracksher vb.
fracture

fufill vb.
fulfill

gamberling vb.
gambling

geneology *n.*
genealogy

goobye/tadar *int.*
goodbye

govament *adj. & n.*
government

grievious *adj.*
grievous

growen *vb. (p.p.)*
grown

haitch *n.*
aitch

he's own *pron.*
his

height-th *n.*
height

hellum *n.*
helm

here's two *phr.*
here are two

hone in *phr.*
home in

hostible *n.*
hospital

humbrage *n.*
umbrage

hundret *adj.*
hundred

hyderangea n.
hydrangea

I went phr.
I said

I never phr.
I didn't

I turned around phr.
I said

I sore it phr.
I saw it

I've rang vb.
I've rung

I rung vb. past
I rang

I've gone phr.
I said

ice-cream comb n.
ice-cream cone

icelated adj.
isolated

igzillary adj. & n.
auxiliary

imminent adj.
eminent/prominent

ingine n.
engine

insinuendo n.
innuendo/insinuation

inter-esting *adj.*
interesting

intergestion *n.*
indigestion

intermediatries *n. (pl.)*
intermediaries

intraveneously *adj.*
intravenously

irregardless *adj. & adv.*
regardless

itinery/itinry *n.*
itinerary

Janry *n.*
January

jest *adj. & adv.*
just

jew *n.*
dew

jewel *n.*
duel

judicial *adj.*
judicious

knowen *vb. (p.p.)*
known

laying (down) *vb.*
lying (down)

learned *n.*
taught

124

lend *n.*
loan

lenth *n.*
length

letcher *n.*
lecture

libry/libery *n.*
library

mahogamous *adj.*
monogamous

mandareen *n.*
mandarin

manerfacture *n. vb.*
manufacture

maximun *n. & adj.*
maximum

me *poss. pron.*
my

medium strip *n.*
median strip

menestration *n.*
menstruation

mingerling *vb.*
mingling

minimun *n.*
minimum

minuet *(lettuce) n.*
mignonette

mirrow *n.*
mirror

mischievious *adj.*
mischievous

miyon miwlyon *n.*
million

munce *n. (pl.)*
months

mute point *phr.*
moot point

muted *vb. (p.p.)*
mooted

nasturtians *n. (pl.)*
nasturtiums

nasturtiums *n. (pl.)*
aspersions

nelegible *adj.*
negligible

nelly *adv.*
nearly

nothink/nuffink *n. adj. & adv.*
nothing

nucular *adj.*
nuclear

obstroperous/obstropulos *adj.*
obstreperous

127

of a night phr.
at night

ony adv.
only

opporchunity n.
opportunity

or right adv.
all right

orderment n.
ornament

orf adv. prop. n. & int.
off

outside of n. adj. adv. & prop.
outside

ow (own) poss. pron.
our (own)

owers n. (pl.)
hours

pacifically adv.
specifically

pantomine n.
pantomime

paps/praps adv.
perhaps

particuly adv.
particularly

pasgetti n.
spaghetti

pavalova *prop. n. & cake*
pavlova

penist *n.*
pianist

pentathalon *n.*
pentathlon

perculator *n.*
percolator

Perf *prop. n.*
Perth

perogative *n.*
prerogative

pervent *vb.*
prevent

phenomenum *n.*
phenomenon

pickernick *n. vb.*
picnic

pitcher *n.*
picture

pleese force *n.*
police force

plutonic *adj.*
platonic

prade *n. vb.*
parade

preshume *vb.*
presume

proberly/probly *adv.*
probably

pronounciation *n.*
pronunciation

proprietary *n.*
propriety

proscribe *vb.*
ascribe

pry minister *n.*
prime minister

punkin *n.*
pumpkin

pursoo *vb.*
pursue

quaterzone
cortisone

ramsack *vb.*
ransack

raw sewerage *n.*
raw sewage

raw-plug *n.*
rawlplug

rawredge *n.*
raw-edge

reconise *vb.*
recognise

refrectory *n.*
refectory

refute *vb.*
reject

reguly *adv.*
regularly

relevation *n.*
revelation

renumeration *n.*
remuneration

132

reservor *n.*
reservoir

restrong *n.*
restaurant

revebrations *n. (pl.)*
reverberations

revelant *adj.*
relevant

rhododendrum *n.*
rhododendron

riseling *n.*
riesling

rooly *adv.*
really

samwich *n.*
sandwich

sawring *vb.*
sawing

Scotch *adj.*
Scottish

scrip *n.*
script

script *n.*
scrip

secetry/secertary *n.*
secretary

self-opiniated *adj.*
self-opinionated

semellon *n.*
semillon

Seri Lanka *prop. n.*
Sri Lanka

sex *n. (pl.)*
sects

sheath of flowers *phr.*
sheaf of flowers

shock exorber *n.*
shock absorber

showen *vb. (p.p.)*
shown

simily *adv.*
similarly

somethink/sumpthink *n. pron. & adj.*
something

stastistic *n.*
statistic

stomick *n.*
stomach

strenth *n.*
strength

subsidary *n.*
subsidiary

succeed *vb.*
secede

Surface Paradise *prop. n.*
Surfers Paradise

susposed/esposed vb. (p.p.)
supposed

sussinct adj.
succinct

sustificate n.
certificate

Synney prop. n.
Sydney

tar exp.
thanks

tea n.
dinner

tempeture n.
temperature

temprally adv.
temporarily

tempry adj.
temporary

tenderhooks n.
tenterhooks

than what conj.
than

that good phr.
so good

there's two phr.
there are two

torturous adj.
tortuous

trate n.
trait

triffic adj.
terrific

typewriter n.
typewriter

umberella n.
umbrella

unfortuney adv.
unfortunately

unequivocably adv.
unequivocally

unindated vb. (p.p.)
inundated

unrule adj.
unreal

veecle n.
vehicle

vetinary adj.
veterinary

vinegarette n.
vinaigrette

vunerable adj.
vulnerable

watercrest n.
watercress

woite woine n.
white wine

woe to go *phr.*
go to whoa

would of *vb. (cond.)*
would have

youse *pron.*
you

yuge *adj.*
huge

yumorous *adj.*
humorous

yuman *adj. & n.*
human

x-eray *n.*
x-ray

zakly *adv.*
exactly

pacifically *adv.*
specifically

fowl swoop *phr.*
fell swoop

a la naturel *Fr. phr.*
au naturel